Big Little Book On Terraform

Contents

Introduction

Hi there and welcome to the Big Little Book on Terraform. This book was written with both the new IT recruit and the seasoned IT professional in mind, but with a view to aid fast recall of information without having to lift a four hundred page tome!

As well as condensing detailed technical facts, it is accompanied with useful hints and diagrams to help the concepts and understanding of the ideas stand out. Handy for those work or interview situations where there's just not enough time to filter out the pertinent information from all that text.

Take care and happy reading.

U V Omos

What is Network Automation?

This is the utilisation of programming/coding and provisioning platforms to build networks and infrastructure without the need for human intervention. It mainly removes the need to manually carry out repetitive tasks, letting computers do the work instead.

This book focuses on the use of programming and tools to automate the provisioning and configuration management of devices.

Provisioning vs Configuration Management

Provisioning is the creation and implementation of resources. But that is where it stops. If a service has been provisioned and then needs changing, a provisioning tool will simply destroy the current service and create it again.

A configuration management tool also creates and implements resources. But if these resources need changes, a configuration management tool doesn't destroy the resource but instead modifies its current state so that it's new state fits the stipulated requirement.

This book will look at Terraform as a *provisioning* tool.

Let's crack on with looking at Terraform.

What Is Terraform?

Terraform is a provisioning tool that can be used to deploy services under a configuration management tool. In itself *Terraform is not a configuration management tool* and should be used along other tools that carry out such tasks.

It is just used for creating or destroying instances of resources such as servers.

Terraform CLI

The following arguments are supplied with the Terraform executable.

- apply
- console
- destroy
- fmt
- get
- graph
- import
- init
- output
- plan
- providers
- push
- refresh
- show

- taint
- untaint
- validate
- version
- workspace
- debug
- force-unlock
- state

Below is an example of a command that will simply build an instance of a devices as specified by any Terraform scripts saved in the current working folder.

```
terraform apply
```

- Actual-Variable-Value-Settings.tfvars

---

4. Show the Current Terraform Plan (optional)

This creates and shows the plan that will be implemented using the current folder's .tf configuration file and the gridlockaz.tfvars variables.

```
terraform plan -var-file gridlockaz.tfvars
```

---

5. Run the Terraform Script

This applies the plan that will be implemented using the current folder's .tf configuration file and the gridlockaz.tfvars variables.

```
terraform apply -var-file gridlockaz.tfvars
```

Setting Up a Terraform Project

Directory Structure

You can create directories in line with your infrastructure.

For example, a network orchestration project could have the following folders on a *nix platform.

/var/terraform/netproject/accesspoints
/var/terraform/netproject/switches
/var/terraform/netproject/firewalls
/var/terraform/netproject/routers

You could then put the relevant Terraform .tf and .tfvars files in each folder and run the Terraform executable against them to build the environment.

Note that a .tfvars files is not compulsory.

Configuration Components

As mentioned in previous sections, Terraform uses a.tf file format to store its configurations.

Each Terraform project's set of scripts must have the following sections.

- Providers
- Resources

These can be in the same or different.tf file or different files. These are described further below.

Providers

This refers to the *organisation or technology providing the resource being provisioned* e.g AWS, GCP, Microsoft Azure, etc.

A provider configuration would be similar to the following. This would be saved in a file, for instance in provisiontest.tf.

```
provider "aws" {
     access_key = "YOUR-ACCESSKEY"
     secret_key = "YOUR-SECRETKEY"
     region = "us-east-1"
}
```

The access key and secret key would be the AWS credentials needed to build an instance on the account.

Resources

This refers to *the type of provider resources that need provisioning* e.g. Linux server, AWS VPC. Each resource has a type and this type is linked to a provider. For example, an AWS EC2 instance is a type linked to Amazon's "aws" as a provider.

A resource would be configured as follows. This would be saved in a file, for instance in resourcetest.tf.

```
resource "aws_instance" "gridlockaz" {
    ami = "ami-2757f631"
    instance_type = "t2.micro"
}
```

A Basic Configuration File

A provider and a resource are all that is needed to run a Terraform script.

Putting this all together for a complete configuration file for a script that builds a t2.micro AWS instance called gridlockaz would be as follows.

The access key and secret key would be the AWS credentials needed to build an instance on the account.

This would be saved in a file, for instance in scripttest.tf.

```
provider "aws" {
     access_key = "xxxxxxxxxx"
     secret_key = "xxxxxxxxxx"
     region = "us-east-1"
}

resource "aws_instance" "gridlockaz" {
     ami = "ami-2757f631"
     instance_type = "t2.micro"
}
```

This would build an AWS virtual machine using the Amazon Machine Image (AMI) ami-2757f631and the instance type t2.micro.

You can get the exact syntax for various providers at the Terraform website. The direct link for examples of providers' configurations at the time of writing is shown below.

https://www.terraform.io/docs/providers

Find out further information about AWS at the following link.

https://aws.amazon.com

Modules

Modules are a means of creating reusable code and resources. These can take inputs and outputs and an API interface to your modules. This ensures the code is DRY (Don't Repeat Yourself) and reusable.

Check out the *Terraform Module Registry* online for verified community modules.

Modules are a way of creating self-contained reusable configurations that can be managed as a group. The following is an example of a module definition for an AWS VPC.

This would be saved in a file, for instance in moduletest.tf.

```
module "vpc" {
    source = "./vpc"
    name = "web"
    cidr = "1.1.1.1/24"
    public_subnet = "2.2.2.2/24"
}
```

This looks just like a resource without a type. They must have a *source*. This tells Terraform where to find the module's source code. This could be locally or online e.g. on GitHub.

A module can be duplicated with different names and the same source in a configuration e.g. if needed for various customers or departments with varying IP configuration settings.

Location Examples

Location examples are typically written in the following format.

terraform-aws-modules/vpc/aws

An example of a Git location is shown below.

git::https://github.com/abc ref=production

Terraform Registry modules with a blue tick are verified and from a Hashicorp partner. An example is shown below.

```
module "consul" {
  source = "hashicorp/consul/aws"
  version = "0.1.0"
}
```

A few registry module examples are as follows.

- GitHub
- Bitbucket
- Generic Git
- Generic Mercurial
- Amazon Bucket

Further information on these is shown below.

GitHub

The following clones over SSH.

```
module "consul" {
  source =
"git@github.com:hashicorp/example.git"
}
```

The following clones over HTTPS.

```
module "consul" {
  source = "github.com/hashicorp/example"
}
```

Using GitHub as the source enables versioning.

Bitbucket

```
module "consul" {
  source = "bitbucket.org/hashicorp/terraform-
consul-aws"
}
```

Generic Git

```
module "vpc" {
  source = "git::https://example.com/vpc.git"
}
```

```
module "storage" {
  source =
"git::ssh://username@example.com/storage.git"
}
```

Generic Mercurial

```
module "vpc" {
   source = "hg::http://example.com/vpc.hg"
}
```

Amazon Bucket

```
module "consul" {
   source = "s3::https://s3-eu-west-
1.amazonaws.com/examplecorp-terraform-
modules/vpc.zip"
}
```

Creating Modules: Summary Steps

- Create a new folder e.g *submod*
- In the new folder add an empty file main.tf to the folder
- Go back to the root folder and create a file with the following contents
  ```
  module "submod" {
  source = "./submod"
  }
  ```
- Run the 'terraform get' command to synchronise modules

Using Modules

These need variables as INPUTS and they can generate corresponding OUTPUTS.

E.g.

Module Structure

The structure of each module folder would be as follows.

- Root module: folder containing the module
- README
- LICENSE
- Main.tf, variables.tf, outputs.tf
- Nested modules: saved in modules/
- Examples: saved in the examples/ folder

These module configurations consist of the following components.

- Variables/Variable Definitions
- Resources
- Outputs

These are described further below.

Variables/Variable Definitions

```
variable "testing" {
     description = "this is a test variable"
}
```

Each variable must be set for a Terraform script to be applied and saved in a .tfvar variable file.

Resources

Variables would be referred to within a Terraform resource as shown below.

```
resource "aws" "internet" {
    vpc_id ${aws_vpc.tfb.id}"
    tags name = "${var.name}-gw
}
```

These variables would exist in the earlier described .tfvar variable file.

Note that the specific provider to use can be set in the module using a *meta tag* as shown below.

```
module "vpc" {
    source = "./vpc"
    name = "web"
    cidr = "1.1.1.1/24"
    public_subnet = "2.2.2.2/24"
    providers = {"aws" = "aws-usc1"}
}
```

Outputs

These are effectively the API response from using the module.

```
output "showdata" {
    value = "${aws_public_subnet.id}"
}
```

Note that this setting isn't just for modules but can used anywhere.

The module needs updating/synchronisation before it can be used.

```
terraform get -update
```

Backends

These are optional configurations that can determine how state is loaded and the way in which commands and arguments such as `terraform apply` are executed. These can be used to save state remotely and enhance teamworking by enabling various teams' access to the same state information.

Creation, changes and removal of configurations update the backend when the `terraform init` command is launched on the CLI.

Functions

Backends have the following functions.

- Storing state
- API state locking (optional)

Types

The types of backends are listed below.

- Standard: covers state management and locking
- Enhanced: covers standard and remote commands

Each of these backends has the following types.

Standard Backends

- artifactory
- azurerm
- consul
- etcd
- etcdv3
- gcs
- http
- manta
- s3
- swift
- Terraform Enterprise

This is an example of an etcd backend in the main Terraform (.tf) configuration.

```
terraform {
  backend "etcd" {
    path     = "path/to/terraform.tfstate"
    endpoints = "http://one:4001 http://two:4001"
  }
}
```

This effectively saves the backend state in the path shown.

Each of these backends has a similar configuration that can be used in .tf files.

Enhanced Backends

- Local
- Remote

A local backend saves the state on the local system whilst a Terraform Enterprise account is needed to store a remote backend.

Configuration

- Back up the terraform.tfstate file
- Add the following configuration to the config terraform section.
  ```
  terraform {
    backend "consul" {
      address = "demo.consul.io"
      scheme  = "https"
      path    = "example_app/terraform_state"
    }
  }
  ```

Plugins

Terraform plugins are written in the Go programming language. In fact, all providers and provisioners in Terraform are plugins and are all written in Go.

Plugins are out of this book's scope and are just defined here for awareness.

Provisioner

A provisioner copies files from the Terraform executable's location to a remote server. These can be used to daisy chain resource provisioning in the order in which the provisioner resources are specified. These are as follows.

Connection Types

These can be SSH or WinRM connections. Examples are shown below.

```
# Copies the file as the root user using SSH
provisioner "file" {
  source      = "conf/myapp.conf"
  destination = "/etc/myapp.conf"

  connection {
    type     = "ssh"
    user     = "root"
    password = "${var.root_password}"
  }
}
```

```
# Copies the file as the Administrator user using WinRM
provisioner "file" {
  source      = "conf/myapp.conf"
  destination = "C:/App/myapp.conf"

  connection {
    type     = "winrm"
    user     = "Administrator"
    password = "${var.admin_password}"
  }
```

}

OS Requirements

Note that on *nix systems, ssh should be installed/available on the device executing the provisioning command.

On Windows systems, WinRM should be installed/available.

Provisioner Types

There are a few types of provisioners as follows.

- Chef: provision and run Chef client on remote machine
- Connection:
- File: copies files from local to remote
- Habitat: installs Habitat and loads its services (needs curl, tee and setsid)
- Local-exec: run commands on local machine
- Null_resource:
- Remote-exec: run command on remote resource after it is created
- Salt-masterclass: provisions salt-state built machines

It is advisable to have curl on both the local and remote hosts where relevant.

File Provisioner

Data sources are defined with the resources. They could typically have a data source from the template provider.

Remote Execution Provisioner

This runs scripts and commands on a remote instance in any of the following modes

Single script
List of scripts in specified order
List of commands in specified order

Provisioner Example

```
resource "aws_instance" "web" {
 # Copies the gridlockaz.conf file to /etc/gridlockaz.conf
  provisioner "file" {
    source      = "conf/gridlockaz.conf"
    destination = "/etc/gridlockaz.conf"
  }

  # Copies the string in content into /tmp/file.log
  provisioner "file" {
    content     = "ami used: ${self.ami}"
    destination = "/tmp/file.log"
  }

  # Copies the configs.d folder to /etc/configs.d
  provisioner "file" {
    source      = "conf/configs.d"
    destination = "/etc"
  }

  # Copies all files and folders in apps/app1 to
D:/IIS/webapp1
  provisioner "file" {
    source      = "apps/app1/"
    destination = "D:/IIS/webapp1"
  }
}
```

Cascading Provisioners

This means that a provisioner can be configured in multiple files with each provisioner giving different types of access e.g. for a root account.

A resource or provisioner can have a connection block that overrides the default connection.

Terraforms Commands

A full list of Terraform commands was shown earlier, but we will go through the main commands used on a day-to-day basis in this section.

The direct link for examples of providers' configurations at the time of writing is shown below.

https://www.terraform.io/docs/commands

Some of these are listed below.

```
terraform init
terraform plan
terraform apply
terraform graph
terraform output
terraform destroy
terraform show
```

Each of the main commands listed will now be reviewed.

terraform init

This is used to review and initialise all of the Terraform files in the current directory. It will check the .tf and .tf.json files to ensure their syntax and variable settings are correct. Any changes are updated in the .tfstate file.

terraform plan

This checks the configure files and based on their contents plans out the intended deployment with a view to flushing out any potential errors.

terraform apply

This applies the configurations to the configured nodes.

The following command bypasses interactive authentication.

```
terraform apply auto-approve
```

terraform graph

This builds a map/diagram of the configurations showing each of the resources (to be) built as a result of the configurations.

This diagram can be viewed in applications such as X that can take .dot and .svg input and build graphs onscreen using them.

terraform output

This shows the output of the terraform apply command.

terraform destroy

This deletes all of the infrastructure being managed under the configured files in the current folder. This should be used with care for obvious reasons.

terraform show

This shows output from the help files for Terraform commands.

Working Example of a Complete Terraform Installation

The following is an example of a terraform script used to deploy an AWS instance.

It consists of the following files all saved in the same folder.

- Instance.tf
- Provider.tf
- Securitygroup.tf
- Vars.tf
- Terraform.tfvars

These are shown below with variables shown in double curly brackets for convenience i.e. {{ }}.

Please ensure that you replace the double curly bracketed variables with actual values before using these scripts.

For clarity the following variables are using in these scripts.

{{ MACHINE_NAME }} an arbitrary machine name for this virtual machines
{{ HOST_NAME }}
{{ MACHINE_NUMBER }} an arbitrary machine number for this virtual machines
{{ INSTANCE }} an arbitrary instance name for this virtual machines
{{ SECURITY_GROUP }} name of the AWS security group to create

{{ AMI }} the type of Amazon Machine Instance to build

The syntax of each of the files is shown in the following sections.

Instance.tf

```
resource "aws_key_pair" "{{ MACHINE_NAME }}-{{
MACHINE_NUMBER }}-thiskey" {
key_name = "{{ MACHINE_NAME }}-{{
MACHINE_NUMBER }}-thiskey"
public_key =
"${file("${var.PATH_TO_PUBLIC_KEY}")}"
}


resource "aws_instance" "{{ INSTANCE }}" {
ami = "${lookup(var.WIN_AMIS,
var.AWS_REGION)}"
instance_type = "t2.medium"
key_name = "${aws_key_pair.{{ MACHINE_NAME }}-
{{ MACHINE_NUMBER }}-thiskey.key_name}"
user_data = <<EOF
<powershell>
net user ${var.INSTANCE_USERNAME}
'${var.INSTANCE_PASSWORD}' /add /y
net localgroup administrators
${var.INSTANCE_USERNAME} /add

winrm quickconfig -q
winrm set winrm/config/winrs
'@{MaxMemoryPerShellMB="300"}'
winrm set winrm/config
'@{MaxTimeoutms="1800000"}'
winrm set winrm/config/service
'@{AllowUnencrypted="true"}'
```

```
winrm set winrm/config/service/auth
'@{Basic="true"}'

netsh advfirewall firewall add rule
name="WinRM 5985" protocol=TCP dir=in
localport=5985 action=allow
netsh advfirewall firewall add rule
name="WinRM 5986" protocol=TCP dir=in
localport=5986 action=allow

net stop winrm
sc.exe config winrm start=auto
net start winrm
</powershell>
EOF

connection {
type = "winrm"
timeout = "5m"
user = "${var.INSTANCE_USERNAME}"
password = "${var.INSTANCE_PASSWORD}"
}
vpc_security_group_ids=["${aws_security_group.
{{ MACHINE_NAME }}-{{ MACHINE_NUMBER }}-{{
SECURITY_GROUP }}.id}"]

}

output "ip" {

value="${aws_instance.{{ INSTANCE
}}.public_ip}"

}
```

Provider.tf

```
provider "aws" {
access_key = "${var.AWS_ACCESS_KEY}"
secret_key = "${var.AWS_SECRET_KEY}"
region = "${var.AWS_REGION}"
}
```

Securitygroup.tf

```
resource "aws_security_group" "{{ MACHINE_NAME
}}-{{ MACHINE_NUMBER }}-{{ SECURITY_GROUP }}"
{
name="{{ MACHINE_NAME }}-{{ MACHINE_NUMBER }}-
{{ SECURITY_GROUP }}"
egress {
from_port = 0
to_port = 0
protocol = "-1"
cidr_blocks = ["0.0.0.0/0"]
}
ingress {
from_port = 0
to_port = 6556
protocol = "tcp"
cidr_blocks = ["0.0.0.0/0"]
}
tags {
Name = "allow-RDP"
}
}
```

Vars.tf

```
variable "AWS_ACCESS_KEY" {}
variable "AWS_SECRET_KEY" {}
variable "AWS_REGION" {
default = "eu-west-2"
}
variable "WIN_AMIS" {
type = "map" default = {
eu-west-2 = "{{ AMI }}"
}
}
variable "PATH_TO_PRIVATE_KEY" { default = "{{
MACHINE_NAME }}-{{ MACHINE_NUMBER }}-thiskey"
}
variable "PATH_TO_PUBLIC_KEY" { default = "{{
MACHINE_NAME }}-{{ MACHINE_NUMBER }}-
thiskey.pub"
}
variable "INSTANCE_USERNAME" { default = "{{
USERNAME }}" }
variable "INSTANCE_PASSWORD" { }
```

Terraform.tfvars

```
AWS_ACCESS_KEY="{{ ACCESS_KEY }} "
AWS_SECRET_KEY="{{ SECRET_KEY }} "
INSTANCE_PASSWORD="{{ PASSWORD }}"
```

Update all of the variable values with required information, save all of the earlier listed files to the same folder, change the current working directory to this folder and run the following command for the scripts to build a new AWS Windows virtual machine at the AWS account whose credentials were specified in the tfvars file.

```
terraform plan && terraform apply
```

This will create an Windows 2012 AWS virtual machine using the t2.medium image in the account with owns the supplied credentials.

It will also create the relevant public and private keys that will be used to authenticate the virtual machine and copy the public key to AWS.

Managing Scripts After Deployment

Terraform.tfstate File

This file is saved automatically in the local folder on running the 'terraform apply' command and contains the state of the resource after it has been created. Do not delete this file as Terraform will then not be able to determine the deployment state of the .tf files in the current folder.

Using GitIgnore On TFState Files

These files should not be added to Git as they contain certain information that should not be kept in repositories for security reasons.

The following steps ensure that certain files are ignored when updating a Git repository. Git must be installed for the 'git' commands to run.

```
echo gridlockaz.tfstate >> .gitignore
git add .gitignore
git commit -m "add a relevant comment here"
```

Conclusion

That's it for now folks. Hopefully this has been a useful 'introduction' or 'reminder' of some key concepts and will continue to be useful to you as a serious networking professional. We are constantly striving to enhance the Big Little Book series so let us know if there are any topics you would like to see in future editions of this book. That's it for now, let us know if there's anything you would like added to the next edition of this book by sending an email to info@gridlockaz.com.

Thanks for reading and wishing you all the best in your career pursuits.

Take care.

U V Omos

Printed in Great Britain
by Amazon

60255748R00024